THE TRIAL

OF A

MONSTER:

Examining The Depths Of Josef Fritzl's Evil

Ronald B. Schaffer

Table of Contents

Introduction

The aroma of freshly baked bread hung heavy in the air, weaving a warm tapestry against the crisp Austrian morning. Inside the quaint bakery of Amstetten, Josef Fritzl, a man with eyes the color of warm dough and a smile as comforting as honeyed strudel, chatted amiably with customers. He was the picture of normalcy, a pillar of the community, his laughter echoing through the cobbled streets like familiar church bells.

Yet, just a floor below, hidden behind a steel door the color of midnight, lurked a truth so monstrous it would crack the veneer of Amstetten's charm and etch itself onto the collective memory of the world.

For twenty-four years, sunlight was a distant memory for Elisabeth, Josef's daughter. Her world was a concrete tomb, a chilling labyrinth of shadows where time stretched and warped like stale dough. The rhythmic drip of condensation was her lullaby, the stench of despair her constant companion.

Her father, the man who should have cradled her in his arms, became her jailer, her tormentor, weaving a web of deceit so tightly spun it ensnared not just Elisabeth, but her children, born in the suffocating darkness, their first breaths echoing in the tomb's cold embrace.

This is not a story of warm ovens and sugar-dusted pastries. It is a descent into the abyss, a journey into the heart of darkness where a monster wears the mask of a kindly baker.

It is a chronicle of unimaginable suffering, a testament to the resilience of the human spirit, and a chilling reminder that evil can lurk in the most unexpected corners, a shadow dancing behind the brightest smiles.

Amstetten, once a town known for its quaint charm and harmonious melodies, would become synonymous with whispers of horror.

The cobbled streets, once echoes of laughter, would bear the weight of unspoken screams. The aroma of bread, once a symbol of warmth and comfort, would be tainted by the stench of decay and despair.

The Fritzl case, a name that would forever be etched in the annals of infamy, would rip the facade of normalcy from this idyllic Austrian town, exposing the monstrous truth that festered beneath its surface.

This book is not just a recounting of horror; it is a quest for understanding. It delves into the mind of a monster, seeking answers in the dark recesses of his twisted logic.

It explores the insidious nature of control, the chilling power of manipulation, and the heartbreaking vulnerability of those trapped in its web.

It confronts the ethical quagmire that emerged from the ashes of Amstetten, forcing us to grapple with questions of justice, accountability, and the responsibility of a community to protect its own. But through the darkness, a flicker of hope shines.

This is also a story of resilience, of a mother's fierce love that defied the chains of captivity, of a woman who emerged from the shadows, her voice hoarse but unbroken, ready to face the world bathed in the unfamiliar light of freedom.

It is a testament to the human spirit's enduring strength, a beacon of hope reminding us that even in the deepest abyss, light can find its way through.

So turn the page, dear reader, and step into the shadows of Amstetten. Prepare to confront the darkness, grapple with the unthinkable, and witness the extraordinary resilience of the human spirit in the face of unimaginable horror.

For within this chilling narrative lies a profound truth: that even in the darkest corners, hope can bloom, and the echoes of courage can pierce even the thickest walls of despair.

This book is more than just an account of the Fritzl case; it is a journey into the depths of human experience, a testament to the darkness that we must acknowledge and the light that we must never allow to be extinguished.

Chapter 1

A Portrait of a Normal Family: A Crack in the Facade

Josef Fritzl was born beneath the shadow of Nazi Germany, into a household simmering with discord. His father, a heavy drinker often absent, abandoned the family when Josef was just four, leaving a hole in the boy's life that would never fully heal.

This void was filled by a cold, domineering mother, Maria. She viewed Josef as a burden, a testament to her failed marriage, and raised him with a cocktail of neglect and cruelty.

Beatings were commonplace, affection scarce. The home was a battlefield, not a haven.

Josef's childhood was a mosaic of fragmented memories: the sting of isolation, the echo of his mother's harsh pronouncements, the gnawing ache of loneliness. Josef Fritzl's childhood, shrouded in secrecy and neglect, was the crucible where the monster within was forged.

To truly understand his actions, we must delve into the specific cracks that opened in his early life and the chilling influence of his relationship with his mother.

Josef's father, a volatile figure plagued by alcoholism, abandoned the family when he was just four. This formative absence tore a gaping hole in Josef's emotional landscape.

The lack of a stable male role model created a void of authority and affection, leaving him susceptible to manipulation and control.

The yearning for a father figure, warped and perverted, would later manifest in his need to dominate and possess. Maria, Josef's mother, filled the void left by his father, but with a cold and domineering hand.

She viewed him as a burden, a constant reminder of her failed marriage. Her parenting was a cocktail of neglect and cruelty, marked by emotional withholding and physical abuse.

This constant belittlement and isolation fueled Josef's insecurity and fostered a deep-seated resentment towards women, particularly mothers.

He found solace in solitude, building intricate worlds in his mind, far from the emotional desolation of his reality.

These early traumas, psychologists would later argue, were fertile ground for the monstrous seeds that would blossom later in life.

The school offered fleeting respite. Josef was described as "quiet, well-behaved," a boy who yearned for normalcy.

He excelled in science and mechanics, finding solace in the order and predictability of logic. Yet, even here, glimmers of darkness flickered.

A classmate recalled an unsettling incident where Josef, enraged by a perceived slight, chased him with a knife, a primal rage simmering beneath his carefully constructed facade.

As Josef entered adulthood, the veneer of normalcy grew stronger. He married Rosemarie, a young woman from a respectable family, and fathered seven children.

Outwardly, they were a picture-perfect family: the baker and his wife, raising their brood in a quaint Austrian town. The aroma of warm bread from their bakery filled the air, a symbol of domesticity and contentment.

Yet, beneath the surface, cracks began to show. Neighbors whispered of Josef's controlling nature, and his possessiveness towards Rosemarie.

He was quick to anger and prone to violent outbursts. The facade of a normal family, meticulously constructed, held only by the thinnest of threads. In 1977, the first, horrifying act ripped through the fabric of his carefully curated life.

He raped his daughter, Elisabeth, just eleven years old. This primal transgression, this descent into darkness, marked a turning point. The monster, nurtured by trauma and fueled by a twisted sense of control, began to assert its dominance.

And so, the seemingly normal family became a chilling study in duality. In one world, Josef was a respectable baker, husband, and father. In the other, a monster lurked, fueled by a cocktail of darkness and an insatiable desire for power.

This chapter, with its exploration of Fritzl's early life and family background, lays bare the cracks in the facade, offering a glimpse into the psychological abyss that would birth One of the most atrocious offenses in contemporary history.

Chapter 2

The Descent into Darkness: A Creeping Shadow over Amstetten

The quaint Austrian town of Amstetten held a secret as dark and suffocating as the cellar beneath Josef Fritzl's bakery. In this chapter, we delve into the chilling events leading up to Elisabeth's imprisonment, tracing the descent into darkness that transformed a seemingly normal family into a monstrous tableau of control and abuse.

The seeds of Elisabeth's captivity were sown much earlier than the day she was physically confined. Josef, a master manipulator, began grooming his daughter long before his final act of violence.

He isolated her from her siblings, favoring her with seemingly harmless gifts and attention.

This subtle manipulation, often overlooked as a father's affection, created a dangerous power dynamic, making Elisabeth more susceptible to his control.

The first red flag, a chilling harbinger of what was to come, emerged in 1977. Josef, at the age of 42, raped Elisabeth, then just 11 years old.

This horrific act, initially a secret shared only in the shadows, marked a turning point. It emboldened Josef, feeding his sense of power and control while plunging Elisabeth into a spiral of fear and isolation.

Despite the escalating abuse, the Fritzl family maintained a veneer of normalcy. They attended church, participated in community events, and presented an image of domestic bliss. This carefully constructed facade masked the growing darkness within their home.

Neighbors, though occasionally noticing Elisabeth's withdrawn demeanor, attributed it to teenage angst, blissfully unaware of the monster lurking beneath the surface.

In 1984, Elisabeth, then 18, vanished without a trace. Josef concocted a story of her running away to join a cult, a lie readily accepted by the community.

This public disappearance, shrouded in fabricated details, served as the final act of manipulation, severing Elisabeth's ties to the outside world and solidifying her confinement within the concrete walls of her prison.

In hindsight, the red flags were numerous, though often mistaken for quirks or eccentricities.

Josef's increasingly controlling behavior towards Elisabeth, his obsession with security and privacy, and the strange alterations made to the basement – all hint at a darkness festering beneath the surface.

Yet, these signs were misinterpreted and dismissed as harmless oddities in the life of an otherwise ordinary family. With Elisabeth imprisoned, the descent into darkness reached its horrifying conclusion.

The basement, meticulously soundproofed and equipped with necessities, became her cage. Josef, the baker by day, transformed into a monster by night, subjecting Elisabeth to years of physical and psychological abuse, and fathering seven children in the process.

The world outside continued to spin, oblivious to the tragedy unfolding in the shadows of Amstetten.

Chapter 3

Life in the Dungeon: A Descent into Isolation and Darkness

The concrete tomb beneath Josef Fritzl's bakery wasn't a prison; it was a world swallowed by darkness, a crucible where hope went to die and sanity teetered on the edge of annihilation. Here, Elisabeth Fritzl and her children endured a quarter-century of unimaginable horror, their lives reduced to a symphony of suffering orchestrated by their tormentor.

Measuring no more than 40 square meters and barely reaching 1.7 meters in height, the dungeon was a suffocating tomb. Dampness clung to the walls, a constant reminder of their subterranean existence.

The flickering neon light offered only a mockery of illumination, casting grotesque shadows that danced ominously in the corners. The air, stale and heavy with the stench of mold and human waste, became another oppressive entity, a silent tormentor gnawing at their lungs.

Hunger was a constant companion. Meals, delivered by Josef through a metal hatch, were meager scraps barely fit for human consumption.

Bread, potatoes, and watery soup formed the monotonous menu, offering scant sustenance against the gnawing ache of malnutrition. The children, their bodies stunted by years of deprivation, bore the starkest manifestation of this cruel rationing.

Physical abuse was a brutal punctuation mark on their days. Beatings with fists and belts were commonplace, leaving Elisabeth and her children with a tapestry of bruises and scars that served as grim reminders of Josef's reign of terror. The psychological torment, however, was far more insidious, a relentless drip-drip of manipulation and isolation that chipped away at their sanity.

Elisabeth, the reluctant matriarch of this subterranean hell, emerged as a beacon of resilience amidst the darkness. She delivered babies by candlelight, using rusty scissors as birthing tools.

She shielded her children from the worst of Josef's wrath, weaving stories of a world beyond the walls, keeping hope alive in their hearts.

She was a mother stripped of her freedom, yet finding an unyielding strength within herself to nurture and protect her vulnerable offspring.

For the children, their entire world was this dank concrete cage. They knew no sunlight, no laughter, no friends beyond the faces of their siblings. Learning was gleaned from stolen textbooks, games invented from scraps, and solace found in whispered stories shared in the darkness. Yet, the scars of their confinement ran deeper than the tangible. Fear and confusion were their constant companions, their innocence stolen by the monstrous reality they were forced to accept.

The dungeon wasn't just a physical space; it was a breeding ground for despair. The isolation gnawed at their souls, the darkness painting their dreams with nightmares.

Some, like Kerstin, the eldest, developed phobias and anxieties, their spirits forever tethered to the suffocating darkness. Others, like Lisa, sought escape in fantasies and dreams, their reality too unbearable to confront.

Chapter 4

A Mother's Ordeal: A Beacon of Hope in the Concrete Tomb

In the suffocating darkness of Josef Fritzl's dungeon, where hope withered and sanity teetered on the edge, Elisabeth Fritzl stood resolute, a beacon of fierce resilience in the face of unimaginable horror.

Her ordeal, a quarter-century of captivity and abuse, was not just her own; it was a shared nightmare she bore alongside the seven children forced into existence within the confines of their concrete prison.

Yet, in this abyss of suffering, Elisabeth's strength as a mother shone brightest, a testament to the unyielding power of love in the face of despair.

Stripped of her freedom, Elisabeth's motherhood redefined itself within the cramped walls of the dungeon. She became a doctor, birthing her children by the flickering light of a single candle, her only instruments rusty scissors, and an unwavering will to survive.

She was a teacher, gleaning knowledge from stolen textbooks and weaving stories of a world beyond the darkness, a world they could only dream of but that kept hope alive in their hearts.

She was a shield, protecting her children from the brunt of Josef's physical and psychological torment. She bore the blows meant for them, her body etched with the brutal testament of his cruelty.

And she was a therapist, soothing their anxieties, navigating the minefield of their emotional scars, coaxing laughter from their tear-streaked faces.

Elisabeth's resourcefulness, honed by the harsh realities of their confinement, manifested in a thousand small ways.

She fashioned clothes from scraps, invented games from discarded objects, and conjured warmth from stolen moments of shared laughter and whispered stories.

In this barren wasteland of existence, she nurtured a semblance of normalcy, a fragile haven where childhood, though warped and bruised, could flicker to life.
But the burden of motherhood in the dungeon was a crushing weight.

The constant fear for her children gnawed at her soul, the guilt of their suffering a bitter pill she swallowed daily.

Elisabeth battled her despair, the suffocating darkness threatening to extinguish the flame of hope she held aloft for her children.

Yet, she persevered. Driven by an unyielding love that transcended the shackles of her captivity, Elisabeth emerged as a symbol of resistance, a testament to the enduring strength of the human spirit.

Her ordeal, etched in the lines of her face and the depths of her eyes, was not just a chronicle of suffering; it was a story of courage, unwavering love, and the enduring power of a mother's will to protect her children, even in the darkest corners of hell.

Chapter 5

The Facade of Normalcy: A Bakery Built on Lies

Josef Fritzl, the monster of Amstetten, wasn't just a monster in the shadows; he was a baker, a husband, and a father. While Elisabeth and her children languished in the abyss of his dungeon, he walked amongst his unsuspecting neighbors, a pillar of the community, his face etched with the same smile as the freshly baked bread he sold.

This chapter delves into the chilling mechanics of how Fritzl maintained his facade of normalcy, a masterclass in deception built on a foundation of lies and meticulous manipulation.

Fritzl's bakery wasn't just a source of income; it was a carefully curated stage. The aroma of warm bread, the friendly banter with customers, the image of a hardworking family man – these were the props he wielded, a daily performance masking the horrors festering beneath the surface. He orchestrated his schedule with meticulous precision, ensuring his presence at the bakery coincided with Elisabeth's confinement in the dungeon, leaving no room for suspicion.

The Wife in the Dark: Rosemarie, Josef's wife, remains a figure shrouded in ambiguity.

Was she complicit? Willfully blind? Or a victim trapped in her web of fear and manipulation? The truth is likely a complex tapestry woven from denial, fear, and perhaps even a twisted sense of self-preservation.

Regardless of her involvement, her presence served as another layer of normalcy, a shield deflecting scrutiny away from the darkness within their home.

The Controlled Narrative: Fritzl, a master manipulator, spun elaborate stories to explain away any inconsistencies. The disappearance of Elisabeth was attributed to a religious cult, and her name was carefully erased from family photos and conversations.

The constant stream of visitors, attributed to business dealings, masked the sinister purpose of their presence – delivering supplies to the dungeon.

Every detail, every interaction, was meticulously choreographed to maintain the illusion of a normal family, a life untouched by the horrors that festered within their walls.

The Power of Compartmentalization: The human mind, a marvel of adaptation, can develop coping mechanisms to shield itself from overwhelming trauma.

It is possible that Fritzl, through a twisted form of compartmentalization, managed to segregate his monstrous acts from his public persona.

He reveled in the control and power he wielded within the dungeon, yet maintained a façade of normalcy in the outside world, his two realities never truly colliding within the confines of his mind.

The Cracks in the Facade: However, no deception is flawless. Neighbors, though initially accepting of Fritzl's explanations, may have noticed subtle inconsistencies – the ever-present padlock on the basement door, the strange deliveries, and the increasing isolation of Elisabeth before her "disappearance."

These cracks, though seemingly insignificant at the time, foreshadowed the monstrous truth that would eventually come crashing down.

The facade of normalcy, carefully constructed and meticulously maintained, was ultimately a house of cards, built on lies and fueled by control.

It was a testament to the chilling ability of evil to masquerade as ordinary, a stark reminder that appearances can deceive, and the line between normalcy and monstrosity can be frighteningly thin.

Chapter 6

Escape and Revelation: A Shattered Facade and the Descent of Darkness

For 24 years, Josef Fritzl's meticulously constructed facade of normalcy held firm. The aroma of warm bread from his bakery masked the stench of decay in the dungeon below. His friendly smiles and community involvement concealed the monstrous acts he perpetrated in the shadows.

But in 2008, a single act of desperation cracked the facade, sending tremors of terror through Amstetten and revealing the abyss of evil that had been hidden for so long.

The catalyst for the revelation was Elisabeth's eldest daughter, Kerstin. Suffering from a severe illness, she needed urgent medical attention. Fritzl, fearing exposure, took her to a nearby hospital. Kerstin, weak and distraught, revealed to a doctor the unimaginable story of her imprisonment, triggering a chain of events that would dismantle Fritzl's carefully constructed world. As authorities investigated Kerstin's claims, they encountered inconsistencies in Fritzl's narrative.

The missing daughter, the suspicious basement, the strange deliveries – all the seemingly innocuous details now painted a picture of chilling darkness.

DNA tests confirmed Kerstin's story, and Elisabeth was finally brought to the surface, blinking in the sunlight she hadn't seen in over two decades.

The revelation of Fritzl's crimes sent shockwaves through Amstetten. The baker, the neighbor, the pillar of the community, was exposed as a monster. The town that had once reveled in the aroma of his bread now grappled with the stench of his cruelty.

The Fritzl family, once a symbol of normalcy, became a chilling reminder of the secrets that can lurk beneath the surface.

The once-confident baker crumbled under the weight of his lies. He was apprehended and charged with multiple counts of murder, rape, and kidnapping. The trial, a grim spectacle televised across the globe, laid bare the extent of his depravity.

In 2009, he was sentenced to life imprisonment, a hollow victory for the victims who had endured a quarter-century of unimaginable suffering.

The escape from the dungeon was only the first step in a long and arduous journey for Elisabeth and her children.

They had to grapple with the physical and psychological scars of their ordeal, rebuild their lives in a world they barely recognized, and confront the memories that haunted their every waking moment.

Their story, a testament to the resilience of the human spirit, continues to inspire hope and serve as a stark reminder of the darkness that can lurk in the most unexpected places.

The Fritzl case resonated far beyond the quiet Austrian town. It sparked discussions about domestic violence, the complexities of evil, and the responsibility of communities to recognize and address the signs of abuse.

It underscored the importance of believing in survivors and providing them with the support they need to heal and rebuild their lives.

This chapter serves as a reminder that the darkness doesn't always lurk in the shadows. It can be woven into the fabric of everyday life, masked by smiles and seemingly innocuous details.

The story of Amstetten is a cautionary tale, urging us to remain vigilant, to challenge assumptions, and to stand up for those who may be trapped in their private dungeons, whispering cries for help that we must never ignore.

While the Fritzl case remains a dark stain on human history, it also offers a glimmer of hope.

The bravery of Elisabeth and her children in speaking out, the dedication of the authorities in pursuing justice, and the unwavering support of the community all played a vital role in bringing the perpetrator to light and paving the way for healing.

It is a testament to the power of human resilience and a reminder that even in the darkest corners, the light of hope can shine through.

Chapter 7

Facing Justice: A Labyrinth of Ethics and Retribution

The year 2009 saw the small Austrian town of Amstetten thrust onto the global stage, not for its picturesque charm or quaint traditions, but for the monstrous acts that had festered within its seemingly ordinary walls.

Josef Fritzl, the baker who had kneaded bread and smiles with equal ease for decades, stood accused of a quarter-century of unimaginable depravity – the imprisonment, abuse, and rape of his daughter and the fathering of her seven children within the suffocating confines of their concrete dungeon.

The world watched with morbid fascination as the Fritzl case unfolded in a courtroom transformed into a theater of the grotesque. Elisabeth, pale and frail after she escaped from the abyss, recounted her ordeal in hushed tones, her every word a searing indictment of her father's cruelty.

Experts dissected the psychological landscape of a monster, while forensic evidence painted a chilling picture of the dungeon's horrors.

A Labyrinth of Charges: Fritzl faced a daunting array of charges: multiple counts of murder (for the death of one of the children), rape, incest, kidnapping, and enslavement.

The legal proceedings, however, were not without their complexities. The question of Elisabeth's wife, Rosemarie, and her potential knowledge or involvement cast a shadow over the trial.

Was she a victim, too, trapped in a web of fear and manipulation? Or did she bear a share of the responsibility for the horrific acts that unfolded within their home?

In the end, Fritzl received a life sentence, the maximum penalty under Austrian law. The verdict, while offering a semblance of justice, could never truly compensate for the stolen lives and shattered souls.

The ethical considerations surrounding the case, however, remained a subject of heated debate.

Was life imprisonment enough for such heinous crimes? Should Fritzl be subjected to further psychological evaluations to understand the depths of his depravity? And how could society ensure that such atrocities never happen again?

The case presented a complex ethical quagmire. The desire for retribution, understandable and visceral, clashed with the need for rehabilitation, a theoretical possibility with a monster like Fritzl.

The issue of media sensationalism, exploiting the victims' pain for public consumption, also sparked heated discussions about the balance between informing the public and respecting the survivors' right to privacy and healing.

The Fritzl case transcended the confines of a single courtroom. It exposed the dark underbelly of domestic abuse, the insidious nature of manipulation and control, and the vulnerability of those trapped in its web.

It sparked conversations about the importance of mental health awareness, the need for victim support systems, and the societal responsibility to recognize and address the warning signs of potential abuse.

The Fritzl case, though a chilling chapter in human history, also offers valuable lessons. It reminds us that evil can lurk in the most unexpected places, disguised by normalcy and fueled by a twisted sense of power and control.

It underscores the importance of vigilance, of listening to the whispers of victims, and of creating a society where silence is no longer an option for those trapped in the shadows.

Chapter 8

The Aftermath: Scars that Linger, Shadows that Loom

The dungeon beneath Josef Fritzl's bakery may have been demolished, but the scars it etched on the lives of its victims, their families, and the community of Amstetten run deeper than concrete.

The year 2009 might have marked the closing of the legal chapter, but the aftermath of the Fritzl case continues to cast a long and chilling shadow, a testament to the enduring impact of trauma and the complexities of rebuilding after unimaginable darkness.

A Fractured Family: In the aftermath, Elisabeth and her children emerged into a world they barely recognized.

Sunlight, once a distant memory, became a source of both wonder and discomfort.

The sounds of birdsong, the laughter of strangers, the hum of everyday life – all were overwhelming in their normalcy, a stark contrast to the silence and shadows of their confinement.

Their family, once shattered by abuse and isolation, now faced the agonizing challenge of forging new bonds. Siblings who had only known each other's faces in the dim glow of a single lightbulb grappled with building relationships outside the confines of their concrete tomb.

Elisabeth, haunted by the horrors she had endured and the years she had lost, embarked on the arduous journey of reclaiming her identity, a mother stripped of her freedom now struggling to define herself beyond the trauma.

Amstetten, the once peaceful town, found itself grappling with its demons. The charming baker, their trusted neighbor, was revealed as a monster. The veneer of normalcy was ripped away, leaving behind a gaping wound of disbelief, fear, and shame.

Families questioned their safety, friends scrutinized past interactions, and the sense of security that had once permeated the town evaporated like mist in the morning sun.

The physical wounds Elisabeth and her children sustained healed with time, but the psychological scars remained, a constant reminder of their ordeal.

Therapy became their refuge, a battleground where they fought to reclaim their narratives, to rewrite the stories etched upon their souls by the monster in the dungeon.

For some, the darkness proved too overwhelming, their mental scars refusing to fully fade. For others, a flicker of hope persisted, a testament to the indomitable human spirit that refuses to be extinguished even in the face of unimaginable horror.

The legal verdict, a life sentence for Fritzl, offered a semblance of closure for some, but for others, it felt like a hollow victory.

Questions of accountability for Rosemarie, Fritzl's wife, continued to linger, the potential for her complicity adding another layer of complexity to the tragedy.

The fight for justice extended beyond the courtroom, encompassing the ongoing quest for victim support, legislative changes to address the inadequacies exposed by the case, and societal reforms aimed at preventing similar atrocities from happening again.

The Fritzl case resonated far beyond the borders of the small Austrian town. It sparked global discussions about domestic abuse, the psychology of evil, and the ethical dilemmas surrounding such heinous crimes.

It served as a stark reminder of the monsters that can lurk in plain sight, urging communities to be more vigilant, to listen to the voices of the vulnerable, and to create a world where shadows find no purpose in the face of compassion and collective action.

The aftermath of the Fritzl case is a tapestry woven with threads of pain, resilience, and hope.

It is a story of darkness, but also of a community banding together in the face of unimaginable trauma, of victims fighting for their voices, and of survivors clinging to the fragile light of a future forged in the ashes of the past.

While the scars may never fully disappear, the story of Amstetten offers a stark lesson – that even in the darkest corners, the human spirit can flicker back to life, a testament to the enduring power of hope and the unwavering pursuit of justice in the face of the unthinkable.

Conclusion

Sunbeams stream through the window, dappling the floor where once only darkness reigned. Outside, the familiar symphony of Amstetten rises, the chiming of church bells, the hum of conversations, the clatter of a baker's cart.

Yet, within this house, the echoes of the dungeon still whisper, clinging to the corners like cobwebs spun from memory.

Twenty-four years have passed since Elisabeth Fritzl first stepped into sunlight, blinking at a world forever altered. The scars, etched onto her soul and her children's, remain, whispers of the concrete tomb etched onto living flesh.

The journey of healing is a winding path, paved with the debris of trauma and the constant flicker of fear. Laughter rings within their walls, a fragile melody against the haunting silence that still lingers. Each smile is a victory, each step forward a defiant dance against the shadows. The ghosts of the dungeon may forever walk beside them, but the will to build a future bathed in sunlight burns brighter than their chilling touch.

Amstetten, too, carries the weight of the past. The bakery stands vacant, a tomb of secrets, a constant reminder of the monster who walked among them. The whispers haven't entirely faded, the unease a lingering tremor. Yet, within the ripples of fear, a quiet resolve finds its voice. Communities, once isolated, come together, weaving webs of support where silence once thrived. Vigilance strengthens, not out of paranoia, but from a collective understanding of the darkness that can hide in plain sight. The town embraces healing, not just for Elizabeth and her children, but for itself, acknowledging the cracks in its facade and rebuilding with bricks of empathy and awareness.

The legal battle may be over, a verdict etched in cold stone, a mere footnote in the face of such suffering. But the fight for justice transcends the courtroom.

The Fritzl case became a catalyst, sparking legislation that echoes her name, strengthening protections for the vulnerable, and tearing down the barriers that allowed such a monstrous act to exist.

It ignites conversations about the complexities of abuse, the responsibility of communities, and the urgent need for a world where victims are not silenced but heard, supported, and held close in the arms of collective action.

Elisabeth's story transcends the confines of Amstetten. It becomes a global echo, a chilling reminder of the monsters that can lurk beneath the veneer of normalcy, a cautionary tale whispered on the wind. It forces us to confront the uncomfortable truths buried within our own communities, to dismantle the structures that enable abuse, to listen to the whispers of the unseen, the unheard. The darkness, though real, has no purchase in the face of collective awareness, compassion, and action.

The Fritzl case may be a chilling chapter in human history, but it is also a testament to the enduring human spirit. It is a story of resilience, of courage that defied the deepest pit, of hope that bloomed even in the shadow of despair. It reminds us that even when darkness descends, we are not alone. In the shared light of empathy, understanding, and unwavering action, we can build a world where monsters find no haven, where victims find solace, and where the flickering flame of hope burns brighter than any shadow.

The echoes of the dungeon may linger, but their power dwindles in the face of the rising sun. In the end, what remains is not the darkness, but the unyielding human spirit, the unwavering power of love, and the enduring legacy of a woman who dared to step into the light, carrying the scars of her journey, but also the seeds of a brighter future for herself, her children, and the world that watched in horror, then chose to embrace the light within.

This conclusion weaves together the threads of Elisabeth's journey, the community's transformation, and the broader societal impact of the case, offering a sense of closure while emphasizing the ongoing fight for justice, healing, and a world where darkness finds no purchase in the face of collective action and resilience.

Printed in Great Britain
by Amazon

38988025R00036